Blender Recipes For Weight Loss

C	O	C	O	N	U	T	A	S	Q	D	T	I	A
A	K	E	B	R	O	C	C	O	L	I	T	K	L
Q	A	X	B	H	C	M	J	V	U	G	C	L	M
K	A	L	E	I	O	D	G	I	N	G	E	R	D
C	R	A	S	P	E	R	R	Y	H	F	B	J	S
C	K	Y	O	T	A	V	O	C	A	D	O	L	Q
R	J	S	G	K	S	C	X	B	A	N	A	N	A
J	X	F	O	K	K	A	L	E	B	R	U	S	Q
A	G	U	B	L	U	E	B	E	R	R	Y	F	T
V	J	U	Y	N	Q	X	B	J	T	W	K	S	X
U	P	A	P	A	Y	A	A	P	R	I	C	O	T
G	D	L	N	P	H	P	E	C	A	N	A	S	A
P	Q	H	Y	X	T	E	B	J	M	O	O	E	H
C	U	O	S	O	E	F	V	H	L	W	C	K	L

Blender Recipes For Weight Loss

1/2 cups rice milk
1/2 cups silken tofu
1/3 cups creamy peanut butter
2 fresh bananas

2 cups brewed double strength coffee
1 pint coffee ice cream
6 cups ice
1 1/2 cups skim milk
Whipped cream (optional)
Cinnamon/Chocolate

1/2 cups plain or vanilla yogurt
1 1/2 cups frozen blackberries
1 banana
1/2 bag of frozen blueberries
2 tablespoons blueberry preserves
7 or 8 ice cubes
1 1/2 cups of soymilk

3 small ice cubes
2 apricots
1/2 papaya
1/2 mango
1/2 cups carrot juice
1 tablespoon honey

4 medium bananas
light brown sugar
hazelnuts
1/4 cups milk
1/4 cups dark rum
or hazelnut liqueur
banana liqueur
vanilla syrup
half and half
ice cubes
chopped walnuts
2 ounces whipped cream

- 1 large avocado
- 2 teaspoons condensed milk
- 1 cup ice
- frozen bananas
- 4 to 5 strawberries
- nonfat soy/nut milk
- cardamom
- allspice

- 1 peach, frozen
- 10 blueberries
- 1 cup light vanilla yogurt
- milk
- crushed pecan
- teaspoons salt
- teaspoons vanilla extract

kefir
half a cup of non-fat milk
a frozen banana
peanut butter
some almonds

1 cup blueberry yogurt
2 cups frozen blueberries
1 scoop vanilla whey protein powder
1 scoop blueberry flavoured VegeGreens

5 or 6 frozen banana slices
1 cup frozen fruit
cup vanilla yoghurt
cup milk
1 teaspoon Splenda

1 banana, sliced
1 cup mixed frozen berries (raspberries, blueberries, strawberries)
1 cup milk of your choice

cucumbers
kale
fresh mint
fresh parsley
fresh ginger
1 avocado
1 cup coconut water
juice of 1 lime
udo's, hemp or flaxseed oil
hemp seeds or chia seeds
liquid stevia

1 cup broccoli florets
1/4 of an avocado
1 banana
1 peach
1 cup unsweetened almond milk
1/4 cup ice cubes

cooked navy beans
frozen mango or papaya
soy milk
honey

1 cup frozen strawberries
1/4 cup ricotta
milk
honey

While every precaution has been taken in the preparation of this book, the publisher assumes no responsibility for errors or omissions, or for damages resulting from the use of the information contained herein.

31 BLENDER & MIXER SMOOTHIE RECIPES FOR RAPID WEIGHT LOSS

First edition. July 10, 2017.

Copyright © 2017 Juliana Baltimoore.

Written by Juliana Baltimoore.

Introduction

Thank you for purchasing my healthy smoothies recipes that helped me lose 40lbs over two month.

When I lost my weight I started to juice and blend at the same time. What I did was either juice or blend a couple of times a day and I combined it with eating healthy clean foods for 1 meal and a healthy snack or two throughout the day.

The more smoothies you drink during the day and the less processed foods you consume the more weight you are going to lose.

After having gone through the Smoothie diet with my own smoothie recipes for weight loss (I did it over the time of 2 months), I am feeling so energized and fit.

I had a great experience with this diet and this is why I'd like to share my healthy weight loss smoothie recipes with anyone who would like to lose weight in a quick, delicious and healthy way.

I am also working on a Juicing for weight loss series that you can combine together with these Smoothie recipes for weight loss so that you can enjoy even more variations of these delicious healthy delights that are not only tasty, but they will also make your body lean and clean.

Just one more last tip. These healthy ingredients and nutrients that are inside these smoothies do even become more beneficial to the body and mind if used and consumed in combination with a light yoga workout or any other workout that you prefer.

I always combine it with some Hatha Yoga poses and a daily meditation ritual, but you can use any light workout that you like to do on a daily basis.

Since I have been changing my lifestyle to include healthy smoothies and yoga into my lifestyle, I am fitter than ever before.

Before I had some health issues, stress and sleeping problems, but since I included daily Yoga combined with these healthy smoothies that I am consuming on a regular basis into my lifestyle, I am a new person.

I am so happy that I got started with changing my lifestyle from a common and unhealthy meal plan to one that includes these delicious and healthy smoothies which kind of transformed my life into a balanced, healthy, energized, lean & clean lifestyle!

I am enjoying this lifestyle so much that I decided to motivate and encourage others to get started with these blender recipes for weight loss, too.

Depending on your own goals and preferences, you can either consume them to become a healthier you or you can apply them as a smoothie diet in order to develop a leaner body or to lose some pounds.

Make sure to first consult your doctor or physician to make sure that this diet is a good fit for your own personal situation.

Preparing these healthy smoothies does not take much time out of your schedule, and if you'd like to learn some cool time management tricks that apply to a healthy lifestyle that includes disciplines like yoga and/or meditation then I highly recommend my sister's book series that you can find online as well.

She calls it her Daily Ritual Yoga and Meditation Lifestyle series. You can check it out on the marketplaced by typing in her name: Alecandra Baldec and you will find all her books.

Each smoothie recipe for weight loss includes a list of ingredients that you need to have in order to get started. Each smoothie does not take longer than 5 minute in terms of preparation.

For each Smoothie recipe, simply add all ingredients into a Vitamix or your favorite high-speed blender.

In my case, I love the Nutribullet and it has changed my life.

When you are going to prepare the smoothie make sure to add some water or ice cubes, if needed, to reach your desired thickness. For all recipes, use organic products, fruits and vegetables when possible.

I include exactly the same recipes that helped me lose more than 40lbs over a period of two months. I am constantly improving these recipes and I am constantly adding more recipes to this book in order to update it with my latest proven and tested recipes. Make sure to check back on a regular basis to access the updated version.

I hope you enjoy the book and I hope that you will get lots of inspiration and stimulation out of the book in order to be able to take advantage and be empowered by the fact that you can lose weight very effectively, but also by the fact that these healthy smoothies are helping you tap into some very powerful health and detox benefits.

Remember, each and every recipe and ingredient has its own benefits for weight loss and health!

All you have to do is identify your goal and take your daily action steps. If you follow my model above, you will have the same success with these delicious and healthy smoothies for weight loss.

If you are looking to just become healthier, make sure to integrate more and more of these smoothie recipes into your daily meal plan and if you are looking to lose weight, first check with your doctor and then you can follow my smoothie weigh loss model that I explained above.

Everybody has a different goal and you can consume less or more of these smoothies depending on your personal situation, your goal and your
lifestyle.

One thing is for sure, if you get yourself into the habit of consuming these smoothies, you will empower and transform your body and mind with the result of a healthier, cleaner, fitter and leaner you!

Why You Should Read The Book

You should read this book because in this book you will find superfoods that are very beneficial for your health and they will keep your body lean and clean.

Taking in all these superfoods via smoothies on a daily basis is going to benefit you because you are going to keep your body disease free and best of all drinking these smoothies on a daily basis is keeping the doctor far far away!

These are the 18 secret superfoods and what they can do for your body and mind.

1. Avocado

Promotes the health of your heart

Avocado has wide ranging anti-inflammatory benefits

Avocado supports cardiovascular health

Avocado promotes blood sugar regulation

Avocado has anti-cancer benefits

Avocados contains 18 amino acids that are required to form complete protein that is used more efficiently by your body than proteins that are found in meat foods

Avocados contain more natural fiber than any other fruit, and this high fiber content aids in digestion and total body absorption of nutrients.

Healthy fats found in avocados do raise the "good" cholesterol while lowering the "bad" cholesterol and the triglycerides by 20%.

Avocados contain 35% more potassium than do bananas

Potassium is important because it regulates your blood pressure

Avocados do provide the lutein that is necessary to protect you from age related eye degeneration problems

The anti-inflammatory properties of avocado fruits do prevent and do treat rheumatoid arthritis

Sufficient amounts of oleic acid also do improve your cardiovascular system and do protect you against prostate and breast cancer

Glutathione that is contained in avocados boosts your immune system and does keep your nervous system healthy and fit

Avocado health benefits are also considered one of the nature's most effective moisturizers for the skin

Avocado has shown to increase collagen production of the skin as well as reduce the size and appearance of wrinkles

Avocado Beauty Tips:

Mix the pulp of an avocado and apply it as a masque directly to your face and body skin

If you suffer from sunburn, eczema, dry spots or psoriasis, the healthy fat in avocado protects, repairs and moisturizes your skin

The pulp closest to the avocado skin has the highest concentration of nutrients

Make sure to use this pulp and scrape it off the skin

Apply this pulp directly to the skin for a soft and a supple result

2. Blueberries

These are the benefits of blueberries:
Whole body antioxidant support
Cardiovascular benefits
Cognitive benefits
Blood sugar benefits
Eye health
Anti cancer benefits

3. Coconut

These are the benefits of coconut:
Helps prevent obesity
Improves heart health
High in dietary fiber
Low glycemic index
Reduces sweet cravings
Improves digestion
Quick energy boost

In addition, coconut contains no trans fats, is gluten free,
Non-toxic, hypoallergenic.
It also contains antiviral, antibacterial, antifungal, and
anti-parasitic healing properties.
Coconut helps your overall immune system functions.

4. Ginger
These are the benefits of ginger:
Gastrointestinal relief
Safe and effective relief of nausea
Anti-inflammatory effects
Protection against colorectal cancer
Ginger induces cell death in ovarian cancer cells
Immune boosting action

5. Kale
These are the benefits of kale:
Antioxidant related health benefits
Anti-inflammatory health benefits
Glucosinolates and cancer preventive benefits
Glucosinolates in kale and their detox activating isothiocyanates
Cardiovascular support
Other health related benefits

6. Raspberries
These are the benefits of raspberries:
Antioxidant and anti-inflammatory benefits
Obesity and blood sugar benefits
Anti-cancer benefits

7. Papaya

These are the benefits of papaya:

Protection against heart disease

Anti-inflammatory effects

Promotes digestive health

Immune support

Protection against rheumatoid arthritis

Papaya and green tea in combination prevents prostate cancer

8. Broccoli

These are the benefits of broccoli:

The cancer-inflammation-oxidative stress-detox connection

Anti-inflammatory benefits

antioxidant benefits

broccoli can enhance detoxification

broccoli and cancer prevention

broccoli and digestive support

broccoli and cardiovascular support

9. Apricot

These are the benefits of apricot:

Apricots do protect your eyesight

Apricots do contain nutrients (vitamin A for good vision and it is also a powerful antioxidant, Vitamin A quenches the free radical damage to cells and tissues)

10. Banana

These are the benefits of bananas:
Cardiovascular protection from potassium and fiber
soothing protection from ulcers
improving elimination
protect your eyesight
build better bones with bananas
Bananas do promote kidney health through regular and moderate intake

11. Pecan Nuts

These are the benefits of pecan nuts:
One of the most significant facts of pecan nutrition is that pecans are the best antioxidants
Pecan nuts help preventing coronary heart diseases
Pecan nuts contain vitamin E which is a natural antioxidant that protects blood lipids from getting oxidized
Pecans have cholesterol lowering properties
The plant sterols in pecans have cholesterol lowering characteristics
Pecan nuts do help in weight loss

Pecans help in increasing the metabolic rate of the body and they do improve satiety
Pecans do contain 19 plus vitamins and minerals
Vitamins from the B group, vitamin A, vitamin E, calcium, potassium, folic acid, phosphorus, zinc, magnesium just to name a few
Pecans are rich source of proteins and contain less carbohydrates and zero cholesterol
Pecans are best suited for a sodium restricted diet and for heart patients as well as for people with high blood pressure because they are sodium free

12. Walnuts

Walnuts have cardiovascular benefits
Walnuts help reduce problems in metabolic syndrome
Walnuts are beneficial in treatment of type 2 diabetes
Walnuts have anti-cancer benefits
Walnuts have anti-inflammatory nutrients which is perfect for the support of your bone health
A large amount of walnuts decreases your blood levels of N-telopeptides of type 1 collagen
Walnuts are a desirable food for support of weight loss and for prevention of obesity
Walnuts are unique in their collection of anti-inflammatory nutrients
These nutrients include omega 3 fatty acids
Walnuts also promote anti-cancer benefits

13. Carrots

Carrots have a rich supply of antioxidant nutrients called beta carotene
These delicious orange vegetables are the source not only of beta carotene, but also of a wide variety of antioxidants plus other health supporting nutrients.
Other benefits of carrots:
Antioxidant benefits
Cardiovascular benefits
Vision health

14. Lemon

Lemons are very alkalizing for the body and they do help to restore the balance of the pH
Lemons are rich in flavonoids and vitamin C
Vitamin C works against infections like colds and the flu
Lemons are a wonderful stimulation to your liver
Lemon is a dissolvent of uric acid and other poisons
It is a is a great liver detoxifier
It cleanses your bowels

Lemons increase peristalsis in the bowels

The citric acid in lemon juice helps to dissolve calcium deposits, gallstones and kidney stones

Vitamin C in lemons helps the body to neutralize free radicals that are linked to most types of diseases and aging

Lemon peel contains phytonutrient tangeretin

Phytonutrient Tangeretin has been proven to be effective for brain disorders (Parkinson disease for example)

Lemons destroy intestinal worms

In a condition of insufficient oxygen and breathing problems (mountain climbing, etc.) lemons are very helpful

Some other helpful facts about lemons:

Scurvy is treated by giving 1-2 ounces of lemon juice with water every 2 to 4 hours

Tip:

Mix the juice of one lemon or lime to warm water and drink this mixture first thing in the morning to start your day

15. Peanuts

These are the benefits of peanuts:

Peanuts are a rich source of antioxidants

Heart health benefits

Potentially reduced risk of strokes

Helps prevent gallstones

Protects against Alzheimer and other age related cognitive decline health problems

Lowers risk of weight gain

16. Cinnamon

Anti-clotting actions

Anti-microbial activity
Blood sugar control
Cinnamon's scent boosts the brain function
Calcium and fiber improve colon health and protect against heart disease
Cinnamon is a traditional warming remedy

17. **Pineapple**
    Potential Anti-inflammatory and digestive benefits
    Antioxidant protection and immune support
    Protection against macular degeneration

My Personal Rules For Weight Loss With These Smoothies

Blend a couple of times a day and as long as you plan to apply your Smoothie diet.

Combine it with eating healthy clean foods for 1 meal and a healthy snack or two throughout the day.

Combine your smoothie diet with a light daily workout ritual like Yoga or any other physical activity.

The more smoothies you drink during the day and the less processed foods you consume the more weight you are going to lose.

Don't push yourself too hard. This is a long term strategy and once you reached your dieting goal, make sure to include these healthy smoothies into your daily meal plan in order to stay fit and keep a lean body.

Smoothie 1: Strawberry N'Creams

"Show Me The Smoothies!" Famous Smoothie Quote

If you love tasty smoothies with some strange secret ingredients that are heavenly deliciously then you might consider the Strawberry n'Creams smoothie.

Imagine the best of creams and cheeses combined with some zesty red fruits like strawberries or raspberries.

Pouring the contents of a delightful fruit-cream-cheese platter into your favorite blender (in my case I am using the Vitamix) and whip it all together into a creamy delight.

This cheese, cream and strawberry smoothie drink contains the following ingredients:

Ingredients:

1 cup frozen raspberries or strawberries whatever you prefer or have available

1/4 cup of fresh organic Italian ricotta cheese

1/2 cup of milk or skim milk (depending on your goals and if you are on a diet just use the skim milk and do not add the rich cream)

A Dash of rich tasty cream to swirl this into a creamy and rich tasting delight

Raw organic Honey (optional and to your taste)

Directions:

For all these Smoothie recipe simply follow my 5 minute directions. Add all the ingredients into your Vitamix or similar high-speed blender. Make sure to add fresh spring water. Add as much water as you like in order to reach your desired thickness of the smoothie. For all the smoothie recipes, make sure to use organic products, fruits and vegetables if possible.

Mix the strawberries, the ricotta cheese, the milk and the cream in a blender and swirl it into a creamy texture while adding the raw honey.

In the summer adding some additional ice cubes might be a very refreshing idea. Instead of the ice cubes you can also add some strawberry or raspberry sherbert or ice cream. This is totally optional and depends on your goal. If your goal is to lose weight then just skip the creamy stuff!

Enjoy this refreshing and delicious smoothie!

Smoothie 2: Mango/Papaya Protein Booster

"Next Time, Indiana Jones, it will Take More Than Smoothies to Save You." Famous Smoothie Quote

A combination of healthy and lean making protein and mango is what this smoothie is all about. The Mango Protein booster is perfect if your goal is to follow a lean and clean smoothie diet.

So what is the secret of this protein booster?

Usually smoothies are well known for their high protein content because they do rely on protein powder.

The secret ingredient for the Mango Protein booster, however, is the protein of the cooked navy beans.

You might not like the idea of combining beans into your smoothies, but I am going to change your paradigm quickly after you had your first serving.

I have tested this smoothie with a lot of smoothie lovers before adding it to my collection. I am constantly testing and proving new smoothie recipes that I am gradually adding to my "Tested & Proven Smoothie Recipe Collection"

This one has passed the test because it is not only delicious, but it is such a health treat and perfect for you if you are trying to lose weight with smoothies.

Between the navy beans and the soy milk that is included in this smoothie, you are going to consume around ten to eleven grams of pure protein.

This protein rich smoothie drink contains the following ingredients:

Ingredients:

1/3 cup of cooked navy beans (organic if possible)

1-1/2 cups of frozen papaya or mango

3/4 cups of organic soy milk

2 teaspoons of raw honey (this is optional and try organic raw honey if you can)

Directions:

For all these Smoothie recipe simply follow my 5 minute directions. Add all the ingredients into your Vitamix or similar high-speed blender. Make sure to add fresh spring water if needed. Add as much water as you like in order to reach your desired thickness of the smoothie.

For all the smoothie recipes, make sure to use organic products, fruits and vegetables if possible.

Mix the cooked navy beans and the tropical frozen fruits (mango or papaya) together and process them in your high speed blender until both ingredients are well combined together. Next, add the organic soy milk and the raw honey and continue mixing until everything is combined into a nice and creamy texture. Add ice if needed and to your own liking.

You can adjust the raw organic honey to your preference or you can skip this step if you do not have a sweet tooth or if you are following a strict smoothie diet with unsweetened smoothies.

Smoothie 3: Superfood Greens Shake

1 cup broccoli florets
1/4 of an avocado
1 banana
1 peach
1 cup unsweetened almond milk
1/4 cup ice cubes

"Round up the Usual Fruits and Vegetables."

A fortified and nutritious combination of healthy and lean making superfood greens like broccoli and avocado.

This lean Superfood Greens Shake gets its rich flavor from the nutty tasting avocado.

Who says that vegetables are for lunch and dinner only? This lean green cocktail contains delicious and zesty fruits that are swirled into the greens and this smoothie makes for a perfect wholesome and healthy start of your day so that you do not need to wait for lunchtime to eat these healthy veggies.

This Superfood Greens Shake contains the following

Ingredients:
  1/4 of an organic avocado
  1 cup of organic broccoli florets

1 peeled and organic banana that is already chopped and frozen
1 organic chopped peach or apricot or nectarine
1 cup of unsweetened and organic almond milk
ice cubes to your liking

Directions:

For all these Smoothie recipe simply follow my 5 minute directions. Add all the ingredients into your Vitamix or similar high-speed blender. Make sure to add fresh spring water or ice cubes if needed. Add as much water as you like in order to reach your desired thickness of the smoothie. For all the smoothie recipes, make sure to use organic products, fruits and vegetables if possible.

Mix all the ingredients together and process them with your favorite blender until all of the ingredients are well combined together. Make sure the broccoli is broken down and all the other ingredients are well swirled together in a rich looking creamy texture.

You can add more organic almond milk, water, or ice cubes (depending on your goal) if you like a more fluid and water downed smoothie. If you like you can also add some raw honey or if you are on a smoothie diet and like it sweet you can add a little bit of your favourite sweetener.

Other people love the unsweatened taste!

Smoothie 4: Exotic Coconut & Green Superpower Ginger Smoothie

cucumbers
kale
fresh mint
fresh parsley
fresh ginger
1 avocado
1 cup coconut water
juice of 1 lime
udo's, hemp or flaxseed oil
hemp seeds or chia seeds
liquid stevia

"Not that I loved Ceasar Salads Less, but that I loved Green Smoothies More"

Let's talk about a powerful combination of some fortified, exotic and nutritious superfoods like cucumbers, kale, mint, ginger, coconut water, parsley and more.

The secret ingredient that I use here in order to bring out a rich nutty and exotic tasting flavor is the coconut water.

This is a magical mixture of green and exotic superfoods that are healing in nature. These are ingredients that do not only taste deliciously and exotically, but they will give your body and brain the most nutritious and beneficial nourishment.

Coconut is especially beneficial to help prevent obesity and it improves the heart health.

Coconut is high in dietary fiber, it has a low glycemic index, it reduces sweet cravings, it improves digestion.

It is also a quick energy booster.

In addition, coconut contains no trans fats, it is gluten free and it is non-toxic and hypoallergenic.

It also contains antiviral, antibacterial, antifungal, and anti-parasitic healing properties.

Coconut helps your overall immune system functions.

Ginger is helping with gastrointestinal relief.

Safe and effective relief of nausea and vomiting during pregnancy.

Ginger carries anti-inflammatory effects and helps protect against colorectal cancer.

Ginger induces cell death in ovarian cancer cells and helps boost the immune system.

The Exotic & Green Superpower Smoothie with coconut and ginger contains the following ingredients:

Ingredients:

1-2 organic small cucumbers

3 medium kale leaves (torn)

5 stems of fresh mint

3 stems of fresh parsley

2.5 cm pieces of fresh organic ginger

1 organic avocado

1 cup of organic coconut water

juice of 1 lime

1-2 teaspoons of hemp or flaxseed oil (optional)

1-2 tablespoons of hemp seeds or chia seeds (optional)

2 - 3 drops of liquid stevia

Directions:

For all these Smoothie recipe simply follow my 5 minute directions. Add all the ingredients into your Vitamix or similar high-speed blender. Make sure to add fresh spring water or ice cubes if needed. Add as much water as you like in order to reach your desired thickness of the smoothie. For all the smoothie recipes, make sure to use organic products, fruits and vegetables if possible.

Mix all the ingredients together and process them with your favorite blender until all of the ingredients are well combined together. Make sure the broccoli is broken down and all the other ingredients are well swirled together in a rich looking creamy texture.

Add a little filtered spring water or ice cubes if needed for your desired consistency.

If you like you can also add some raw honey or if you are on a smoothie diet and like it sweet you can add a little bit of your favorite sweetener.

Other people love the unsweatened taste!

Smoothie 5: Rich Berry Screamer

1 banana, sliced
1 cup mixed frozen berries (raspberries, blueberries, strawberries)
1 cup milk of your choice

"Are you Telling Me you Built a Time Machine... out of a Vita-Mix?"

This is a refreshing blend of red, blue and black berries with or without a tropical twist.

It is a great hydratation solution and thirst quencher after a physical workout. The Rich Berry Screamer Smoothie contains the following ingredients:

Ingredients:
1 small organic banana (sliced)
1 cup of mixed frozen berries (raspberries, blueberries, blackberries, strawberries)
1 cup milk of your choice (skim if you are on a smoothie diet)

Tropical orange twist:
Nothing welcomes warmer weather better than the twist of a tropical inspired flavor from pineapples and citrus fruits like oranges and limes.

fresh orange juice
twist of lime or lemon
fresh pineapple juice

Directions:
For all these Smoothie recipe simply follow my 5 minute directions. Add all the ingredients into your Vitamix or similar high-speed blender. Make sure to add fresh spring water or ice cubes if needed. Add as much water as you like in order to reach your desired thickness of the smoothie. For all the smoothie recipes, make sure to use organic products, fruits and vegetables if possible.

Mix all the ingredients together and process them with your favorite blender until all of the ingredients are well combined together. Add a little filtered spring water or ice cubes if needed for your desired consistency.

Add all the ingredients to your blender and puree the mixture until everything is smooth.

Smoothie 6: Vanilla Smoothie Delight

"A Green Smoothie is Worth a Thousand Donuts"

A smoothie might be in the blended beverage category, but a smoothie certainly represent very different aspects.

I love the creamy and delicious taste of a smoothie combined with the health benefits that are offered by a smoothie.

All you need is one very secret ingredient that provides the body and brain with a very powerful health benefit and you can turn a simple milkshake into a nutritious drink.

In the case of the Vanilla Smoothie Delight the secret ingredient are frozen bananas.

Did you know that when bananas are frozen and then blended down, they take on the texture of real ice cream?

Yes, real ice cream but without all the dangerous and sick making additives and fats.

In this case I suggest to buy a whole whack of fresh organic bananas. Let them sit out until they have ripened nicely and are yellow.

They should also show some brown spots, but not have gone quite so far as to be in banana bread making material.

Peel your bananas and slice them so that each slice is about 1.5 to 2 centimeters thick.

Separate all the banana slices and lay them flat in a Ziploc bag and place them like this in your freezer.

Avoid throwing them all in at once. They may be hard to break apart in the quantities that you need them later when they are in a frozen condition. Once you have gone through this freezing process, you will have bananas on hand for your smoothie delights for a good amount of time.

This will be a huge time saver because you can live healthy without having to go to the store and buy fresh bananas all the time.

The Vanilla Smoothie Delight is a great smoothie for beginners and you can play around with it and add some of your own variations.

Make sure to write down your own ingredients that you like to add and your preparation method so that you will remember it later.

I suggest using a site like Evernote or a mobile app where you can quickly take all your notes for later reference.

The Vanilla Smoothie Delight is a great recipe that can act as a base for you to build from and it contains the following ingredients:

Ingredients:

5 or 6 small frozen banana slices (organic if possible)

1 cup of frozen fruits (be creative with your selection like peaches, apricots, strawberries, blueberries, blackberries, raspberries, papaya, mango. Make sure the fruits are frozen because this will add to the creamy texture of the smoothie)

¼ cup of organic vanilla yoghurt

½ cup of milk (skim if you are on a strict smoothie diet)

raw honey or splenda (optional and to your liking)

Directions:

For all these Smoothie recipe simply follow my 5 minute directions. Add all the ingredients into your Vitamix or similar high-speed blender. Make sure to add fresh spring water or ice cubes if needed. Add as much water as you like in order to reach your desired thickness of the smoothie. For all the smoothie recipes, make sure to use organic products, fruits and vegetables if possible.

Mix all the ingredients together and process them with your favorite blender until all of the ingredients are well combined together. Blend the frozen slices of bananas and fruits in your favorite blender or food processor on high speed.

You may need to stop occasionally with the process and return some of the fruits to the base of the blender as the fruits can quickly creep up the sides of your mixing bowl.

Keep blending until all the fruits are broken down into a nice smoothie texture.

Next, add in the vanilla yoghurt, the milk and the raw honey or splenda and continue to mix the drink until thoroughly swirled together.

Transfer your drink to a large glass or two smaller ones and enjoy your delicious and nutritious Vanilla Smoothie Delight.

If you need you can also add some more ice cubes or a little filtered spring water depending on your desired consistency.

Smoothie 7: Purple Power Booster

"All Right, Mr. DeMille, I'm Ready for my Purple Smoothie."

Start your day with a smooth start and loading up on lots of protein is a beneficial way to start your day. This smoothie will also give your muscles the perfect energy they need after a tough workout. This smoothie will provide your body with all the nutrients and fuel that it requires.

This protein packed smoothie is loaded with minerals and vitamins. The amount of protein will give you every ounce of energy that you need each and every day.

The Purple Power Booster contains the following ingredients:

Ingredients:

1 cup of purple/blue or vanilla yogurt (blueberry if possible but you can also use vanilla yogurt)

2 cups of frozen purple fruits like blueberries because they are turning this smoothie into a superfood smoothie

1 scoop of vanilla whey protein powder
1 scoop of blueberry flavored VegeGreens
2 cups of fresh spring water

Directions:

For all these Smoothie recipe simply follow my 5 minute directions. Add all the ingredients into your Vitamix or similar high-speed blender. Make sure to add fresh spring water or ice cubes if needed. Add as much water as you like in order to reach your desired thickness of the smoothie. For all the smoothie recipes, make sure to use organic products, fruits and vegetables if possible.

Mix all the ingredients together and process them with your favorite blender until all of the ingredients are well combined together. Mix all ingredients thoroughly in a food processor or blender.

Add a little filtered spring water or ice cubes if needed for your desired consistency.

Transfer the delicious mix in your favorite smoothie glasses and enjoy.

If you like you can also add some raw honey or if you are on a smoothie diet and like it sweet you can add a little bit of your favorite sweetener.

Some people love the unsweetened and more natural taste.

Smoothie 8: Kefir Peanut Butter Breakfast Smoothie

kefir
half a cup of non-fat milk
a frozen banana
peanut butter
some almonds

"What's in a Name? That which we call a Green Smoothie By any Other Name would Taste as Sweet."

This smoothie contains some beneficial ingredients like almonds and kefir.

Almonds are some powerful miracle workers. They are high in potassium. They also boost your brain activity, reduce the risk of a heart attack and the lower bad cholesterol.

Breakfast is the most important meal of the day.

Make sure not to skip it and consume this powerful breakfast smoothie instead.

This breakfast smoothie is a great way to incorporate nutrition into your day and start your day in an energized and stress-free way.

This smoothie delivers a drink that is full of fiber, good carbs and healthy nutrients.

If your goal is to lose weight, I highly recommend to consume this highly nutritionally dense breakfast smoothie every morning during your smoothie diet. It will help you lose weight, keep lean, stave off illnesses, keep clean and boost energy.

This Kefir Peanut Butter Breakfast Smoothie contains the following ingredients:

Ingredients:
1 cup of kefir
some peanut butter for a nutty rich taste
1 organic small banana
a quarter cup of fresh pineapple
1 cup of organic almond milk (self-made or bought)

Directions:

For all these Smoothie recipe simply follow my 5 minute directions. Add all the ingredients into your Vitamix or similar high-speed blender. Make sure to add fresh spring water if needed. Add as much water as you like in order to reach your desired thickness of the smoothie. For all the smoothie recipes, make sure to use organic products, fruits and vegetables if possible.

Blend a cup of organic kefir, the peanut butter, a ripe banana, a quarter cup of fresh pineapple and one cup of almond milk and swirl it into a smooth silky treat.

Add ice if needed and to your own liking.

You can adjust some raw organic honey to your preference (if it is not sweat enough for your taste) or you can skip this step if you do not have a sweet tooth.

If you are following a strict smoothie diet, I recommend to keep the Smoothie unsweetened.

If the pineapple is ripe, it will add sugar in a natural way.

Smoothie 9: Blueberry Pecan & Vanilla Smoothie

1 peach, frozen
10 blueberries
1 cup light vanilla yogurt
milk
crushed pecan
teaspoons salt
teaspoons vanilla extract

"Round up the Usual Fruits and Vegetables."

The Blueberry Pecan & Vanilla Smoothie is a combination of healthy and lean making superfood ingredients.

So what is the secret of this protein booster?

The secret ingredients are the pecans.

Pecan nuts are a very rich source of energy. Pecans do provide 690 calories / 100 g and do contain health benefitting nutrients: antioxidants, minerals, and vitamins. These are all essential for our wellness.

A regular intake of pecan nuts into your diet plan helps you to decrease total as well as LDL or otherwise known as "bad cholesterol". Eating these nuts does help the increase of HDL or otherwise known as the "good cholesterol" levels in your blood.

Studies also have shown that these healthy compounds that are contained in pecan nuts do in fact help the body remove toxic oxygen free radicals.

This helps protect the body from damages and diseases, infections and cancers.

Pecan nuts do contain anti proliferative properties of ellagic acid which is helping protect the human body from cancers.

Pecan nuts are also an excellent source of vitamin E. Especially rich in gamma tocopherol.

Vitamin E is a powerful lipid soluble antioxidant which is required for maintaining the integrity of cell membrane and Vitamin E helps protect the skin from harmful oxygen free radicals.

These tasty nuts are also a very rich sources of several important B-complex groups of vitamins which are needed for the enzyme metabolism inside the body.

Pecans also do provide a very rich source of minerals like potassium, manganese, calcium, magnesium, iron, magnesium, selenium and zinc.

I recommend to add a hand full of pecans into your smoothies every day to provide your body with sufficient levels of protein, minerals and vitamins.

This protein rich Blueberry Pecan & Vanilla Smoothie contains the following ingredients:

Ingredients:
1 organic peach (frozen)
10-20 organic blueberries (frozen)
1 cup light and fat free organic vanilla yogurt (frozen)
1/2 cup of milk or skim milk
1/2 tablespoon of crushed pecans
1/2 teaspoon of salt
1/4 teaspoons of organic vanilla extract

Directions:

For all these Smoothie recipe simply follow my 5 minute directions. Add all the ingredients into your Vitamix or similar high-speed blender. Make sure to add fresh spring water if needed. Add as much water as you like in order to reach your desired thickness of the smoothie. For all the smoothie recipes, make sure to use organic products, fruits and vegetables if possible.

Put all ingredients into your favorite blender. Blend the mix until your preferred smoothie consistency is reached!

Add ice if needed and to your own liking. You can also add some raw organic honey to your liking or you can skip this step if you do not have a sweet tooth. If you are following a strict smoothie diet, keep the smoothie in its natural and unsweetened form.

Smoothie 10: Avocado Banana Berry Avalanche

1 large avocado
2 teaspoons condensed milk
1 cup ice
frozen bananas
4 to 5 strawberries
nonfat soy/nut milk
cardamom
allspice

"You had me at 'Green Smoothie." Famous Smoothie Quote

A combination of healthy and lean making avocado and strawberries is what this smoothie's secret is all about.

The avocado is a superfood and strawberries are nutrient-rich and packed with antioxidants. Strawberries provide the body with a rich source of vitamin C and a wide range of health benefits.

Strawberries for example help with wrinkle prevention.

The Mayan Indians have a saying: "Where avocados grow, hunger or malnutrition has no friends."

This antioxidant-rich avocado fruit enhances your heart's health, lowers your cholesterol and improves your skin.

Avocados are abundant in minerals and in vitamins.

Avocados contain beta-carotene, vitamins B6, lutein, vitamins C, E and K, zinc, selenium, potassium, folate, glutathione and omega 3 fatty acids.

These are just a few nutrients that are found in a single avocado.

This Avocado Banana Berry Avalanche is the perfect energy booster if your goal is to follow a lean and clean smoothie diet.

This Avocado Banana Berry Avalanche contains the following ingredients:

Avocado Beauty Recipe:

Mash the pulp of the avocado and apply it directly as a masque to your skin. Avocado contains some of the best anti-aging antioxidants and amino acids used in many expensive brand beauty products.

If you suffer from dry skin, spots, sunburn, eczema, or psoriasis, the healthy fat that is contained in avocados is very beneficial for your skin and beauty care because it will heal you from distress, inflammation, dry skin and it will also protect your skin from more damages in the future.

The oil that comes from avocados is the closest to the natural skin oil that is produced by the human body and you can use the avocado pulp and put it on your skin because it has the highest concentration of nutrients.

Just apply it directly to the skin for a soft and supple result.

Ingredients:

1 large organic avocado
2 teaspoons of condensed milk
1 to 1 1/2 frozen organic bananas
5 to 8 frozen or fresh strawberries
a splash of organic non-fat soy or other organic nut milk

a pinch of cardamon
a pinch of allspice
ice cubes

Directions:

For all these Smoothie recipe simply follow my 5 minute directions. Add all the ingredients into your Vitamix or similar high-speed blender. Make sure to add fresh spring water if needed. Add as much water as you like in order to reach your desired thickness of the smoothie. For all the smoothie recipes, make sure to use organic products, fruits and vegetables if possible.

Scoop out the avocado fruit into your favorite high-speed blender. Add 2 teaspoons of condensed milk. Add the ice cubes and blend all together until you get a a semi creamy and silky texture.

Next add the bananas, the strawberries and the organic non-fat soy or nut milk. Finally add the cardamon and the allspice and blend until you reach your desired texture.

I prefer mine very smooth, but some people who tested it preferred a chewable texture of this smoothie. You can always add some more ice cubes or fresh spring water to your liking to get the perfect texture.

Smoothie 11: Hazel Banana Vanilla Walnut Cream Smoothie

4 medium bananas
light brown sugar
hazelnuts
1/4 cups milk
1/4 cups dark rum
or hazelnut liqueur
banana liqueur
vanilla syrup
half and half
ice cubes
chopped walnuts
2 ounces whipped cream

"Hazel Smoothies, I think this is the Beginning of a Beautiful Relationship."

Let's talk about a scrumptious smoothie called the Hazel Banana Vanilla Walnut Cream Smoothie.

It contains some tasty and nutty ingredients like hazelnuts, hazelnut liqueur, banana liqueur, vanilla syrup, and more tasty flavors.

I do not recommend this if you are on a strict smoothie diet, but if you want to treat yourself with a heavenly tasty delight, you must give this one a try.

It contains the following ingredients:

Ingredients:

4 medium bananas (organic if possible and peeled, sliced into 1/2 inch slices)
6 tablespoons of light brown sugar (organic if possible)

1/4 cups of organic hazelnuts
1/4 cup of milk or skim milk
1/4 cups of dark rum or hazelnut liqueur (I prefer the hazelnut liqueur for the nutty taste!)
2 tablespoons of chopped hazelnuts (for the garnish and totally optional)
1 ounce of banana liqueur
1 ounce of vanilla syrup (organic if possible)
2 ounces of half and half
ice cubes
chopped organic walnuts
2 ounces of whipped cream (organic cream if possible)

Directions:

For all these Smoothie recipe simply follow my 5 minute directions. Add all the ingredients into your Vitamix or similar high-speed blender. Make sure to add fresh spring water or ice cubes if needed. Add as much water as you like in order to reach your desired thickness of the smoothie. For all the smoothie recipes, make sure to use organic products, fruits and vegetables if possible.

Place the sliced bananas in a sealed plastic bag and put them back in your freezer and let it freezer for one hour. Place the brown sugar and the hazelnuts in a blender and grind everything together until it is smooth.

Place the frozen bananas, the ice cubes, the milk, the rum or the hazelnut liqueur, the banana liqueur, the vanilla syrup and the half and half in the blender with the brown sugar.

Add ice and blend until smooth

Pour the smoothie drink into your favorite smoothie glasses. Garnish with a topping of whipped cream and sprinkle with chopped hazelnuts and walnuts and serve this tasty delight immediately.

Smoothie 12: The Beta Carotene Energy Booster

- 3 small ice cubes
- 2 apricots
- 1/2 papaya
- 1/2 mango
- 1/2 cups carrot juice
- 1 tablespoon honey

"May the Smoothie be with you...Always"

Let's talk about a powerful combination of some fortified, exotic and nutritious orange superfoods like carrots, papaya, mango and more.

The secret ingredient that I use here in order to bring out a rich nutty flavor of this smoothie is the carrot juice that contains a rich source of beta carotene.

This is a magical mixture of orange colored nutritious and healing vegetables and fruits. These are ingredients that do not only taste deliciously, but they will also give your body and brain the most powerful health benefits.

Carrots have a rich supply of antioxidant nutrients called beta carotene.

These delicious orange vegetables are the source not only of beta carotene, but also of a wide variety of antioxidants plus other health supporting nutrients.

Other benefits of carrots are antioxidant benefits, cardiovascular benefits and vision for your health.

The Beta Carotene Energy Booster Smoothie contains the following ingredients:

Ingredients:
2 apricots (sliced and pitted)
1/2 papaya (frozen in chunks)
1/2 mango (frozen in chunks)
1/2 cups carrot juice
1 tablespoon of raw organic honey
3 small ice cubes
Option:
Fresh orange juice

31 BLENDER & MIXER SMOOTHIE RECIPES FOR RAPID WEIGHT LOSS

Directions:

For all these Smoothie recipe simply follow my 5 minute directions. Add all the ingredients into your Vitamix or similar high-speed blender. Make sure to add fresh spring water or ice cubes if needed. Add as much water as you like in order to reach your desired thickness of the smoothie. For all the smoothie recipes, make sure to use organic products, fruits and vegetables if possible.

Mix all the ingredients in the order listed together and process them with your favorite high speed blender until all of the ingredients are well combined together. Make sure that everything is broken down and all the ingredients are well swirled together in a rich looking orangy colored texture.

Add the raw honey and blend a few more seconds.

Serve the smoothie in a frosted glass.

Option: If you like a thinner consistency, you can add some fresh orange juice. Add the orange juice and blend everything for one more time.

Smoothie 13: The Blackberry Blueberry Blue Preserve Energy Triangle

1/2 cups plain or vanilla yogurt
1 1/2 cups frozen blackberries
1 banana
1/2 bag of frozen blueberries
2 tablespoons blueberry preserves
7 or 8 ice cubes
1 1/2 cups of soymilk

"I love the smell of Purple Smoothies in the morning. It Smells like Victory!"

This smoothie contains some beneficial blue, purple and black ingredients like blackberries, blueberries and blue preserve.

There are an unlimited number of variations for this smoothie because you can use different combinations of jams, preserves and fruits.

Maybe you also want to add some protein powder, organic ground flax seed, nuts or any other additional supplements that you prefer.

You can also substitute the organic apple juice for the organic soymilk to make a tangier and more fruity blend.

This makes for the perfect breakfast smoothie to start your day in an energized and stress free-way.

The Blackberry Blueberry Blue Preserve Energy Triangle Smoothie contains the following ingredients:

Ingredients:

1 1/2 cups of soymilk

3/4 cups of organic apple juice

1/2 cups plain bio or organic yogurt (I prefer to make my own home-made yogurts)

1 1/2 cups frozen blackberries

1/2 bag of frozen blueberries

2 tablespoons blueberry preserves

1 banana

ice cubes

Directions:

For all these Smoothie recipe simply follow my 5 minute directions. Add all the ingredients into your Vitamix or similar high-speed blender. Make sure to add fresh spring water if needed. Add as much water as you like in order to reach your desired thickness of the smoothie. For all the smoothie recipes, make sure to use organic products, fruits and vegetables if possible.

This is super easy to make. Just put all the ingredients into your high-speed blender. Switch the blender to the highest level and blend until you do not hear any ice cubes crunching and until all ingredients are smooth.

Add more ice if needed and to your own liking.

You can adjust the raw organic honey to your preference or you can skip this step if you do not have a sweet tooth or if you are following a strict smoothie diet with unsweetened smoothies.

Smoothie 14: The Coffee'n Cream Cinnamon Smoothie Booster

"I'm Going to Make him a Scrumptious Smoothie he can't Refuse."

The secret here is to enjoy the simple but effective blend of a rich tasting coffee in combination with the organic cinnamon and the taste of intelligence maker number one chocolate.

The Coffee'n Cream Cinnamon Smoothie contains the following ingredients:

Ingredients:
2 cups of brewed double strength coffee (organic if possible)
1 pint of coffee ice cream (your favorite brand, I like mine organic)
1 1/2 cups of milk or skim milk
whipped organic cream (as a topping and if desired)
organic cinnamon and chocolate powder for the garnish
6 cups of ice cubes

Directions:

For all these Smoothie recipe simply follow my 5 minute directions. Add all the ingredients into your Vitamix or similar high-speed blender. Make sure to add fresh spring water or ice cubes if needed. Add as much water as you like in order to reach your desired thickness of the smoothie. For all the smoothie recipes, make sure to use organic products, fruits and vegetables if possible.

Mix all the ingredients together and process them with your favorite blender until all of the ingredients are well combined together. Make sure the broccoli is broken down and all the other ingredients are well swirled together in a rich looking creamy texture.

Blend the coffee, the ice cream, the ice cubes and the milk in your favorite high power blender. Mix everything until you get a smooth texture. Top the smoothie with some whipped cream and add some freshly grounded cinnamon and chocolate powder for the garnish.

If you like you can also add some raw honey or if you are on a smoothie diet and like it sweet you can add a little bit of your favorite sweetener.

Other people love the unsweatened taste!

Smoothie 15: The Peanutbutter Banana Silk

1/2 cups rice milk
1/2 cups silken tofu
1/3 cups creamy peanut butter
2 fresh bananas

"All Great Things are Simple, and Many can be Expressed in Single Words: Freedom, Justice, Honor, Duty, Mercy, Hope, Smoothies."

Let's talk about this scrumptious peanut butter Banana Silk.

Peanuts are not only delicious but they are also very beneficial for the body and brain.

Peanuts are a rich source of antioxidants, they reduced risk of strokes, they help prevent gallstones, they protects against Alzheimer and other age related cognitive decline health problems.

They are very rich in taste and the nutty flavor is popular amongst young and old. As opposed to people's opinion about nuts, they are in fact lowering the risk of weight gain.

The banana is a great combination with peanut butter as Elvis might confirm because he enjoyed his grand mother's and mother's peanut butter and banana sandwiches. He had too many in order to lose weight, but if you are respecting the ingredient list of this recipe, you are going to enjoy the health benefits of peanut butter in combination with bananas.

Here are some of the main health benefits of the banana. Bananas provide a very beneficial cardiovascular protection because of the potassium and fiber.

Bananas do sooth and protect from ulcers. They also improve elimination and protect your eyesight.

They help with your bones and they do promote kidney health.

The Peanutbutter Banana Silk Smoothie contains the following ingredients:

Ingredients:
1/2 cups of organic rice milk
1/2 cups of organic silken tofu
1/3 cups of creamy organic peanut butter
2 fresh organic bananas (sliced and frozen)
2 tablespoons of dark chocolate syrup
ice cubes

Directions:

For all these Smoothie recipe simply follow my 5 minute directions. Add all the ingredients into your Vitamix or similar high-speed blender. Make sure to add fresh spring water or ice cubes if needed. Add as much water as you like in order to reach your desired thickness of the smoothie. For all the smoothie recipes, make sure use organic products, fruits and vegetables if possible.

Blend the organic rice milk, the tofu and the organic peanut butter in your favorite high-speed blender. Add the banana frozen slices, the dark chocolate syrup and the ice cubes.

Blend on high speed until smooth, about 30 to 50 seconds.

Make sure the ingredients are broken down and all the other ingredients are well swirled together in a rich looking creamy and nutty texture.

Add a little more ice cubes if needed for your desired consistency.

If you like you can also add some raw honey or if you are on a smoothie diet and like it sweet you can add a little bit of your favorite sweetener.

Other people love the unsweetened taste!

Smoothie 16: The Golden Delight

1 apple
1 lemon
1 piece fresh gingerroot
ice
filtered water

"We Are such Stuff As Golden Smoothies are Made of..."

Let's talk about a powerful combination of ginger root, lemon and apple.

The secret ingredient is the ginger root her and let's take a look at what the ginger root can do for you.

The anti-inflammatory properties and active principles of the ginger root are thought to provide pain relief in multiple number of ways.

It has the power to stop migraines in their tracks and to ease the aches of arthritis and joint pain.

It also fights ovarian cancer. It seems that ginger has the ability to eliminate the dangerous cancerous ovarian cells. Ginger also seems to slow the progress of bowel cancer.

Ginger also has a boosting effect on the immune system, making you fit and healthy.

Make sure to consume this immune system boosting smoothie drink on a daily basis to stay healthy and clean all year around!

I suggest to drink this smoothie in slow sips and you can keep it near your workspace so you can take a sip throughout the day. If you have trouble sleeping than make sure to only drink this secret ingredient drink in the morning because ginger has a similar characteristic as coffeine.

The peanut butter Banana Silk Smoothie contains the following ingredients:

Ingredients:

1 organic small apple (peeled, cored, sliced)
1 organic lemon (peeled, seeded)
1/2 cups of fresh filtered source water
ice cubes
1 piece of fresh gingerroot (peeled, crushed)

Directions:

For all these Smoothie recipe simply follow my 5 minute directions. Add all the ingredients into your Vitamix or similar high-speed blender. Make sure to add fresh spring water or ice cubes if needed. Add as much water as you like in order to reach your desired thickness of the smoothie.

For all the smoothie recipes, make sure to use organic products, fruits and vegetables if possible.

Mix all the ingredients together and process them with your favorite blender until all of the ingredients are well combined together. Blend all ingredients together until smooth.

Make sure to drink the Golden Delight slowly.

Add a little filtered spring water or ice cubes if needed for your desired consistency.

If you like you can also add some raw honey or if you are on a smoothie diet and like it sweet you can add a little bit of your favorite sweetener.

Other people love the unsweetened taste!

Blender Recipes For Weight Loss Quiz

Blender Recipes For Weight Loss

C	O	C	O	N	U	T	A	S	Q	D	T	I	A
A	K	E	B	R	O	C	C	O	L	I	T	K	L
Q	A	X	B	H	C	M	J	V	U	G	C	L	M
K	A	L	E	I	O	D	G	I	N	G	E	R	D
C	R	A	S	P	E	R	R	Y	H	F	B	J	S
C	K	Y	O	T	A	V	O	C	A	D	O	L	Q
R	J	S	G	K	S	C	X	B	A	N	A	N	A
J	X	F	O	K	K	A	L	E	B	R	U	S	Q
A	G	U	B	L	U	E	B	E	R	R	Y	F	T
V	J	U	Y	N	Q	X	B	J	T	W	K	S	X
U	P	A	P	A	Y	A	A	P	R	I	C	O	T
G	D	L	N	P	H	P	E	C	A	N	A	S	A
P	Q	H	Y	X	T	E	B	J	M	O	O	E	H
C	U	O	S	O	E	F	V	H	L	W	C	K	L

Blender Recipes For Weight Loss

All you have to do is find 12 blender recipes for weight loss ingredients. Use your imagination, read backwards, sidewards, and forwards to find the correct words and associations. Go to the next page to see the correct answers!

Have fun:)

Quiz Answers

Answers:
1. Avocado
2. Blueberry
3. Coconut
4. Ginger
5. Kale
6. Raspberry
7. Lemon
8. Papaya
9. Broccoli
10. Apricot
11. Banana
12. Pecan

Conclusion

My goal with these high-speed blender recipes (in my case I am using the Nutribullet which is my favorite blender) is to give you some delicious blender recipes that are tasty in flavor and that will on the other hand help you with your weight loss goals.

These blender recipes for weight loss and detox are also 5 minute quick to make.

If you drink these nutritious and healthy 5 minute quick lean & clean drink recipes on a daily basis and add a daily workout plan like yoga or any other workout to your daily chores, you will take even more benefits out of your weight loss.

I love these recipes as they help me keep healthy, lean and satisfied.

Each day I will use one or more of these wonderful recipes as a meal replacement for breakfast, lunch or dinner. The best part about using these different drinks is they actually work!

All of the ingredients that you need in order to make these recipes can be found at your local market for less than $9 which makes them affordable, too.

I hope I have delivered and fulfilled my promises and I hope that you are taking action on your own weight loss goals. If you do, you are going to be hooked on this smoothie diet for life!

I encourage you to take note of the many health benefits that come with each individual blender recipe's ingredients.

I also encourage you to take the book/device with you as you go and prepare each individual recipe.

Just keep the book on your mobile device next to your working table and go through one recipe at a time and as you progress. The book is intended to be used as a mental stimulation and to motivate you to take action at the same time.

I tried to make it as effortless, entertaining, inspirational and easy to use and consume as possible.

I hope you will use and consume the content whenever you want to lose some weight and detox your body.

If you really use it as it is intended to be used (use it as you go through the recipes and keep the book close during your preparation time!) it is a very powerful way of discovering the unlimited world of lean & clean high-speed blender smoothie recipes for weight loss!

Remember, all you have to do is open the book and start with the first recipe preparation that you like to get started with. Go through all of them and apply them on a daily basis as you see fit and depending on the health and weight loss benefits that you are looking to achieve.

You just need 5 minutes per preparation to be able to make at least one high-speed blender recipe per day. You can repeat the 5 minute quick preparation time as you see fit during your day.

For example, I am really big on Smoothies because they have helped me beat my Asthma in combination with a daily Yoga workout and therefore I am consuming at least 3 high-speed smoothies during the day when I am at home. It takes me not more than 15 minutes per day with the help of my beloved Nutribullet blender.

In addition to beating my health problems I was able to lose 40 lbs over the period of 2 month.

Everyone has a different goal, but these 5 minute quick and easy recipes that I have been able to perfect with the Nutribullet have certainly made my life easier, disease free, stress-free, cleaner & leaner.

Remember, you can achieve the maximum benefits (weight loss, health, detox, stress free lifestyle, and more) from consuming these high-speed blender (Nutribullet) recipes, too. In combination with a light workout these recipes really do wonderful things for your body and brain and weight loss will be an easy goal with these delicious tasting smoothies if you are going to take action on this!

Once you have achieved your own goal that you are looking to achieve with these amazing high-speed blender recipes by following these easy to follow instructions, you can go ahead and discover even more of these healthy, lean & clean drink ingredients and what they can do for you.

I believe with all the above high-speed blender recipes for weight loss & detox, you will become a lean, fit, healthy and energized person. These smoothies are going to help you become more productive in a stress free way, too.

I am already working on some more clean & lean high-speed blender recipes for you. Once I am done proving and testing them, I will release them as into this blender recipes series.

www.facebook.com/healthysmoothierecipes

About the Publisher

InfinitYou is a hybrid general interest trade publisher. One of the first of its kind InfinitYou publishes physical books, electronic books, and audiobooks in various genres. Our publications are meant to educate, edify and entertain readers of all walks of life from babies to the elderly. Home to more than twenty imprints such as Infinit Baby, Infinit Kids, Infinit Girl, Infinit Boy, Infinit Coloring, Infinit Swear Words, Infinit Activities, Infinit Productivity, Infinit Cat, Infinit Dog, Infinit Love, Infinit Family, Infinit Survival, Infinit Health, Infinit Beauty, Infinit Spirituality, Infinit Lifestyle, Infinit Wealth, Infinit Romance, and lots more.

www.ingramcontent.com/pod-product-compliance
Lightning Source LLC
LaVergne TN
LVHW012126070526
838202LV00056B/5882